T0129756

The Great

WHITE THRONE

Judgment

DR. JOHN THOMAS WYLIE

authorHOUSE®

AuthorHouse™
1663 Liberty Drive
Bloomington, IN 47403
www.authorhouse.com
Phone: 1 (800) 839-8640

© 2019 Dr. John Thomas Wylie. All rights reserved.

No part of this book may be reproduced, stored in a retrieval system, or transmitted by any means without the written permission of the author.

Published by AuthorHouse 11/25/2019

ISBN: 978-1-7283-3764-7 (sc)
ISBN: 978-1-7283-3763-0 (e)

Print information available on the last page.

Any people depicted in stock imagery provided by Getty Images are models, and such images are being used for illustrative purposes only. Certain stock imagery © Getty Images.

This book is printed on acid-free paper.

Because of the dynamic nature of the Internet, any web addresses or links contained in this book may have changed since publication and may no longer be valid. The views expressed in this work are solely those of the author and do not necessarily reflect the views of the publisher, and the publisher hereby disclaims any responsibility for them.

Scripture quotations marked KJV are from the Holy Bible, King James Version (Authorized Version). First published in 1611. Quoted from the KJV Classic Reference Bible, Copyright © 1983 by The Zondervan Corporation.

Scripture quotations marked NIV are taken from the Holy Bible, New International Version®. NIV®. Copyright © 1973, 1978, 1984 by International Bible Society. Used by permission of Zondervan. All rights reserved. [Biblica]

Scripture quotations marked RSV are taken from the Revised Standard Version of the Bible, copyright © 1946, 1952, 1971 by the Division of Christian Education of the National Council of the Churches of Christ in the USA. Used by permission.

American Standard Version (ASV)
Public Domain

The Holy Bible (1959) The Berkeley Version. Grand Rapids, MI.: Zondervan (Used By Permission)

Scripture quotations marked NASB are taken from the New American Standard Bible®, Copyright © 1960, 1962, 1963, 1968, 1971, 1972, 1973, 1975, 1977, 1995 by The Lockman Foundation. Used by permission

Contents

Introduction

"... WHEN THY JUDGMENTS are in the earth, the inhabitants of the world will learn righteousness" (Isa. 26:9 KJV).

The Great White Throne Judgment toward which the unsaved, living and dead, are rushing is the last and final judgment involving humankind. It will occur at the end of the Millennium, which implies that it is at "the end of the world."

During past human history there has been a series of striking judgments, starting with the one articulated on Adam and Eve after they had trespassed (sinned) in the Garden of Eden. Later came the judgment of the flood which concluded the antediluvian era and introduced this present age. Essentially these judgments happened in an astounding pattern of 450-year intervals - 450 being the number of judgment (I Kings 18:19, 40 KJV).

The Twelve Earth Judgments

First Judgment - The Edenic Judgment

Second Judgment - The Flood

Third Judgment - Destruction Of Sodom And Gomorrah

Fourth Judgment - Extirpation Of The Canaanite Nations

Fifth Judgment - Extirpation Of The Amalekite Nation

6th Judgment - The Assyrian And Babylonian Captivities

Seventh Judgment - The Judgment On Christ - This 450-year ended at the advent of the Messiah who took on Himself on the cross the judgment of the believer.

These judgments proceed through the present dispensation and include (8) the ravages of Attila, "the scourge of God" who visited retribution on the Roman Empire; (9) the black death, an epidemic which nearly extirpated humanity during the Middle Ages; (10) the Napoleonic Woe, which transformed Europe into a bloody battlefield; and (11) the judgment of the Day of the Lord which occurs toward the end of the age - the headwaters of which are currently upon us.

The twelfth and last is the Great White Throne Judgment which will come at the end of the Millennium, and will mark the consummation (the completion) of man's 7,000 - year period and the end of the world. The initial eleven are not a subject of this present publication.

You may note (by alluding to the outline) that these judgments fit into a symmetrical pattern in which the captivities that usher in the times of the Gentiles mark the center of the judgment pattern.

The Seventh Judgment Which Fell On Christ

While we can't take note of these 450-year interval judgments at this time, we would pause to note briefly the seventh judgment which fell on Christ at Calvary, for this event is closely identified with our subject.

Extremely critical is the way that the world was spared a judgment at that time. Essentially expressed, it fell on Christ! Barabbas-a kind of blameworthy sinner - was spared, and the judgment fell on the Innocent One (Jesus Christ).

He who knew no sin was made sin for us (II Cor. 5:21). He took the believer's transgressions (sins) and stood in our place in judgment. On the cross Jesus paid the price for our redemption and blotted out the mandates (ordinances) that were against us.

At the same time He triumphed over Satan and the principalities. He defeated the devil so that he has no legal hold on the believer, but by reason of His great redemption man becomes a new creature in Jesus Christ. Summed up, Christ has removed our transgressions (sins), has suffered in our stead, and has taken the judgment which was due us. In this way, "the believer will never stand in peril" of the Great White Throne judgment.

The Judgment Seat Of Christ

There is a judgment which each believer must face, in any case, and that is the one at the judgment seat of Christ. Surely it is a matter which deeply includes the eventual fate of every born-again believer.

The judgment of believers "happens soon after the first resurrection and pertains to rewards."

It is the point at which every believer's works will be tried as by fire to see whether they will endure as being built on gold, silver, and precious stones, or on hay, wood, and stubble, which will be consumed by fire of that searching through judgment:

"Every man's work shall be made manifest: for the day shall declare it, because it shall be revealed by fire; and the fire shall try every man's work of what sort it is. If any man's work abide which he hath built thereupon, he shall receive a reward. If any man's work shall be burned, he shall suffer loss: but he himself shall be saved; yet so as by fire. Know ye not that ye are the temple of God, and that the Spirit of God dwelleth in you?" (I Cor. 3:13-16 KJV).

This judgment of the saints' rewards occurs before the Millennium. The Great White Throne Judgment take place afterward. To this latter we now address ourselves.

Chapter One

The Great White Throne Judgment
(Revelation 20:11, 12)

A GREAT WHITE THRONE shows up in space, and He who sits on that royal throne causes both the earth and the heavens to flee away! Then before the throne appears a tremendous concourse of individuals, not spirits, but living people (human beings) - and the time is the time is "the end of the world!"

This throne which John sees in Revelation is a sharp differentiation to the one he saw in chapter 5. That one had a rainbow over it, demonstrative of promise. Interestingly, the scene of the Great White Throne is exposed naked and without a rainbow.

It depicts only the greatness, the grandness, and the inconceivable, immeasurable power of Almighty God. Its appearance demonstrates that there is nothing gracious or remedial about this judgment. It is retributive and final. The day of probation for mankind (the whole human race) has passed.

On this royal throne sits God, the eternal Godhead. No endeavor is made by John to depict the One who sits on the throne, except to say that before His face, "the earth and the heaven fled away; and there was found no place for them" (Rev. 20:11 NIV).

"The dead small and great stand before God!" This vast or immense concourse of people has quite recently been raised out of hades, the habitation (abode) the dead, where the rich man was of whom Jesus spoke in Luke 16:19-31 KJV.

For thousands of years he and other detainees of this underground jail have anticipated this day, not, notwithstanding, with any glad or happy expectation but with profound foreboding.

They knew they would get their human bodies once more, but only for a limited (brief) time, and with no hope for eternal life. Their considerations, thoughts, along these lines, are only of impending judgment, and of their fate which at this time is to be forever fixed (sealed).

Thus that day has finally arrived! In an instant they approach from the dark passages of hades to stand before the blazing light of the Great White

Throne. These are the unnumbered millions who have lived during progressive or successive periods or times of history, but who shared no part in the first resurrection. They are of the second resurrection. The totality of the event is seen in that not only is it said that hades surrenders its spirits, however the sea additionally surrenders her dead bodies.

Despite where passing may have ended man's natural presence (man's natural existence), the God of all flesh knows where and how to recover both the body and the spirit. What's more, at the time selected He will deliver the individual to stand at the bar that renders eternal justice.

So on that day will come the rulers from their rich tombs, just as the disintegrating tenants of plain graves; yea the rich and poor people, the respectable and the base, the scholarly and the unmindful, the little and the great. They all will approach to stand before God and hear the final verdict, one which man's inner voice (conscience) has officially given him.

They stand as a conspicuous difference to that large number depicted in Revelation 7:9-14 KJV which no man could number. They wear no white robes. They have no palms of triumph. There is no singing - just the horrendous quiet of anticipation of the grave events to come, when every person thus will hear the awesome divine sentence that will spell out his eternal destiny.

This then is the setting of the "Great White Throne Judgment."

Chapter Two

The Resurrection Of The Wicked Dead
(Heb. 9:27)

THE SECOND RESURRECTION WHICH includes the wicked dead of all ages will be a physical resurrection. The human spirits that were made discarnate by death but again will be dressed (clothed) with human bodies. This, it will be noted, is the third transition (real change) of their reality.

The first was their life upon earth in the human body. The subsequent stage started at the hour of physical death. There in the locales of hades the individual got himself an unclothed spirit. The third stage happens at this second resurrection when he again receives a human body, not an immortal one.

There are various circumstances to note in thinking about this event. One thousand years sooner the righteous dead received their glorified bodies. That was the first resurrection. In a moment, in a minute, in a twinkling of an eye that event occurred.

We may assume, in this manner, that the wicked dead at the second resurrection will likewise get their bodies in a same lightning transition. Their old bodies will be reestablished to them with their previous physical resources working again to the full degree.

These people are breathing, living people. While the spirit without the body (just like the instance of the rich man in hades) has resources and feelings comparing to those of the physical body - hearing, sight, taste, feeling, memory, desire, remorse - but the restoration of the body greatly builds the forces and the limits of the individual-either to enjoy bliss, joy, happiness or on the other hand to experience mental anguish, hopelessness, and despair.

Along these lines the second resurrection will have the impact of quickening the resources, making the individual again mindful of his previous conceivable outcomes and possibilities. But, with this mindfulness (awareness) comes the terrible acknowledgment, the awful realization that these powers are lost to him until the end of time.

Maybe in obscurity opening (dark recesses) of hades he may have been able to forget his destiny (his fate). In any case, presently restored to the body, the realization of his terrible fate, his awful doom floods his awareness with overwhelming force, making him suffer in horrifying, agonizing despair.

The wages of sin is death. Also, sin has achieved its work. Having rejected during his lifetime the redemption given by Jesus Christ, man finds as a consequence that this nature has turned out to be irreversibly evil.

For unless if he is redeemed, man should at finally become hopelessly evil. This isn't amazing when we see how depraved men can become in their few years of living upon the earth.

Clearly the thousand of years spent in hades can only bring about the completion of the processes of evil. The despair of the wicked, emerges not just from the fact that they have rebelled against God, and subsequently relinquished (forfeited) their entitlement to everlasting life, however, even were this not so, they understand that they have become an unholy being.

Their debased, perverted nature presently intuitively rebels against God's holiness; therefore they could not be happy beings were they permitted to abide in the purity of God's kingdom.

However they make them fully and completely in common as the righteous. They retain the ability to ache for and want the euphoria (bliss) and joy of the redeemed that they know must always and forever be denied them.

Clearly the judgment of the Great White Throne would have no reason except if the individuals who stood before the bar retain memories of the past. One can comprehend the torment of that memory which reviews the occasions of a squandered, wasted life.

The bound will gnash their teeth futile lament (in vain) as they remember a real life that they lived so casually, so thoughtlessly, so completely unconcerned with all that pertained to their future welfare.

The devilish, the wicked can't obliterate or overlook their past deeds, those they have harmed, their evil conversations, their dishonoring of the name of God, their obscure business bargains - legitimately allowable - however ethically off-base, their joking about and mockery of Christianity, their persecution of God's people.

Despite the fact that man's still, small voice let him know there was a God in heaven with whom he should some time or another figure, and however he know that life was short and death was sure, he proceeded in his ways, unreasonably apathetic regarding the way that "it is appointed to men once to die, after this the judgment" (Heb 9:27 KJV).

Also, presently finally he has gone to the hour of retribution (And now at last he has come to the time of reckoning. Maybe for a minute he could envision himself back in the times of his natural life when salvation was so unreservedly advertised (freely offered). How effectively he could have then respected the voice of still, small voice (conscience). How different his case would be. Be that as it may, it will be past the point of no return, past the point of no return!

Maybe he can recall when he was nearly influenced, when he really considered truly becoming a believer of Jesus Christ. Felix heard Paul preach and trembled, but he let him know, "When I have an advantageous season. I will call for thee" (Acts 24:25 KJV).

The open door passed, and the advantageous season never came. King Agrippa heard the messenger's delicate intrigue and stated, "Almost thou persuadest me to be a Christian" (Acts 26:28 KJV). Almost persuadest, but that was insufficient. How the spirit must denounce itself for so adamantly abandoning light to darkness and from life to death. Furthermore, presently it stands miserable at the judgment bar of a holy and offended God.

The most excruciating situation is that the conscience of man must agree with God. It must agree in the only judgment of the One who sits on the throne of authority. Sin is of such a nature, that it not only offends God, But it irritates, offends man. Of Course, while individuals are occupied with sin, it doesn't appear to be horrible."

Everybody is doing it," they reason to themselves. Be that as it may, sin viewed out of its alluring setting is disgusting, revolting, loathsome and accursed. At the Great White Throne, the offender who once advocated (justified) his course does not do so on the day of judgment.

Satan's Doom
(Rev. 20:10 KJV)

"And the devil that deceived them was thrown into the lake of fire and brimstone,

where the beast and the false prophet are, and shall be tormented day and night forever and ever" (Rev.20:10 KJV).

In spite of the fact that since a long time ago deferred, and however this most outstanding arch-enemy, this adversary of God has set up a frantic fight to dodge his fate, he more likely than not understood that his destiny was inescapable (inevitable) (Rev. 12:12 KJV). Once he was a blessed being who stood high in the counsel of God.

The Scriptures allude to him in Ezekiel 28:12,13, 15 KJV saying, "...Thou sealest up the sum, full of wisdom and perfect in beauty. Thou hast been in Eden the Garden of God... Thou wast perfect in thy ways from the day that thou wast created, till iniquity was found in thee."

Here was eternity's first tragedy. We today are engrossed with the aftereffects of sin upon humankind, so we have not taken full notice of the calamity (catastrophe) that happened in heaven in the distant past.

Lucifer, the son of the morning, was around then without fault. A holy righteous being, he was a close confidant of God and went about as vice-regent of His Kingdom. But he fell, and in his fall he transformed from a beautiful, benign creature into a loathsome, evil, wicked and malevolent being, whose entire intent is now to plunder, topple, despoil and overthrow God's Kingdom.

To this end he has tried to baffle (frustrate) the plan of God and to seduce other creatures of the universe to insubordination (rebellion) and translate them into his very own evil, satanic picture. Everything came about on the grounds that Lucifer enabled pride to enter his heart when he coveted for and looked to lift up himself (exalt himself) into the position the Son of God was to hold:

"How art thou fallen from heaven, O Lucifer, son of the morning! how art thou cut down to the ground, which didst weaken the nations! For thou hast said in thine heart, I will ascend into heaven, I will exalt my throne above the stars of God: I will sit also upon the mount of the congregation, in the sides of the north: I will ascend above the heights of the clouds; I will be like the most High. Yet thou shalt be brought down to hell, to the sides of the pit" (Isa. 14:12-15 KJV).

Such is the result of sin and of the exaltation of self. Satan and the angels that followed him could have been happy beings, envoys of light, and a blessing to God's universe, but instead they chose the way of rebellion.

It is a mystery that would be difficult to comprehend, were it not for the fact that a great many (millions) people likewise endowed with the power of choice are following today the same path of self-will as did Satan.

We need not suppose that in the beginning Lucifer thought to become the devilish, detestable creature that he presently is. At the hour of his fall he was liable (guilty) of one sin, the longing for self-exaltation. He thought he knew better than (superior to) God with respect to how to set up a kingdom.

He would assemble a domain (empire) far more greater than that of the Lord. Be that as it may, when he cut himself off from the Creator (God), the powers of degeneration came into activity, and when they ran their full course, the once angel of light became the monstrous creature of insidiousness, evil he now is, fit uniquely to be annihilated, destroyed.

Now the verse speaking of Satan's fate (his doom) comes just before the passage that relates to the Great White Throne Judgment. Probably this event occurs first, albeit possibly the wicked dead who have chosen to become followers of this enemy of God will be permitted to witness his end.

One thing, is sure; no judgment court (no tribunal) sits for Satan. His judgment has since a long time ago effectively occurred. God has, be that as it may, for a purpose permitted him his liberty for a long season. In spite of the fact that Satan has sought for inside and out to frustrate the divine plan, his insidious, evil activities have only succeeded in helping to bring that plan to fruition.

The Time Of The Great White Throne Judgment (II Pet. 3:8 NIV)

The time of the Great White Throne Judgment can be genuinely fairly fixed. Man's time since the creation of Adam has been roughly 6,000 years long. Biblical scriptures chronology demonstrates that around four millennial, or 4,000 years elapsed from Adam's creation until the coming of the Messiah (The original creation of the universe obviously occurred sometime before Adam).

Since the days of Christ almost 2,000 years have passed. We are currently at the time we write in A. D. 2019. There is little question that inside the following three decades we will perhaps witness the fulfillment of this age.

Despite the fact that this is obvious to the those who observe the fulfillment of the prophecies, researchers, scientists and statesmen perusing the noteworthy signs apart from the Scriptures likewise give the present human civilization just a few more decades to keep running before its breakdown (collapse).

They state, that because of earth contamination, the population explosion, atomic fighting (nuclear warfare, and so on.,) humankind on the cutting edge will devastate (destroy) itself. In this the Bible and science are in completed agreement.

So we have 4,000 years before Christ and around 2,000 years after Christ, making a total of 6,000 years of man's week, as indicated by God's reckoning, which considers about a thousand years as a day.

"But, beloved, be not ignorant of this one thing, that one day is with the Lord as a thousand years, and a thousand years as one day" (II Peter 3:8 KJV).

Then comes the Millennium of a thousand years wherein the saints rule and reign with Christ. Accordingly we have, including the millennial sabbath of 1,000 years, a total of 7,000 years. Since the Millennium must start around 2001 A. D., the part of the plan will be a thousand years after the fact. We understand, therefore, that the Great White Throne Judgment must occur at the end of the third Millennium after Christ.

Chapter Three

The Dead Stand Before God
(Rev. 20:12 KJV)

"I saw the dead, small and great, stand before God..." (Rev. 20:12 KJV).

What a mighty concourse it will be" It was estimated that a crowd of around 4,000,000 accumulated at Cairo for Nasser's memorial service (funeral) - most likely the biggest social occasion of its sort ever. Be that as it may, this extraordinary group of spectators of which we speak must incorporate billions of people.

Only God knows the accurate number. The great of the earth have bragged of their social qualifications, but all are of one size here-kings and queens, princess and potentates, the high and the low, the rich and poor people, the great and the small. Their previous standing has lost all of its significance now.

These are the dead! Unusual that they are spoken of as the dead, for they are likewise spoken of as the living. Revelation 20:5 NIV, anticipating this hour says, "But the rest of the dead lived not again until the thousand years were finished..." The wicked dead are referred to as living again.

The meaning is clear. There are numerous individuals "living" today who are dead even while they live. Paul discussed certain women who were dead even while they lived. "But she that liveth in pleasure is dead while she liveth" (I Tim. 5:6 KJV). Of the backslidden church at Sardis the Lord charged that it had "a name that thou livest, and art dead" (Rev. 3:1 KJV).

By what means can a person be dead while he lives? Man was made in the image of God and is a triune being-body, soul, spirit. In spite of the fact that he has a body, that isn't the most elevated division of his being.

The body only houses the spirit which in addition to other things has the wonderful faculty of being able to commune with God. In this regard man contrasts essentially (differs fundamentally) from the animal kingdom. In his spirit he has a God-cognizance which the animal has not. The animal possesses certain lower faculties of the human being, but not God-consciousness.

An animal eats, drinks, rests, mates, and can participate in different exercises which include the physical faculties (senses). Many people live entirely in the same sensuous realm as the animal. They eat, drink, and have no higher desire than to enjoy the animal pleasures.

They expect to die as an animal and assume that will be the end. They clearly remain unaware of the importance of Christ's words, "Man will not live by bread alone, but by each word that proceedeth out of the mouth of God" (Matt. 4:4 KJV). Having starved their spiritual nature, they live as the brute (the beast, the animal) lives, totally in the physical. At the end of the day, their spiritual nature is dead even while they live.

So it is that in one sense, the dead which come up out of hades to stand before God alive again. They have been resurrected; they again have physical bodies. In any case, their spiritual nature is dead. Along these lines, they are as yet spoken of as "the dead." How awful and horrendous to mull over the awful truth that though these people live again, they are as yet considered "the dead."

The Remorse Of The Wicked
(Heb. 12:16,17 NIV)

That they are members from so huge a concourse can give no solace (comfort) to the wicked dead who are now resurrected. Sinners frequently comfort and console themselves with the idea that despite the fact that their conscience reveals to them they are fouling up doing wrong (sinning), nevertheless a multitude of others are doing likewise.

How often when the invitation is given to sinners to accept Jesus Christ as their Savior, their answer is, "I am okay," or "I am as good as others." But the people who stand at the Great White Throne realize very well indeed they won't be justified on the basis of what others have or have not done, but they will be judged on the basis of their own deeds.

The universal emotion that dominates this huge concourse of the dead should be remorse. Remorse isn't repentance, but instead sad lament (hopeless regret) because of the consequences.

An example of this is the situation of Esau, who sold his birthright without the slightest hesitation (without a second thought), however "afterward, when he would have inherited the blessing, was rejected: for he found no place for repentance, though he sought for it carefully with tears" (Heb. 12:16, 17 KJV). As Jesus said, "There will be weeping and gnashing of teeth," by the lost (Matt. 8:12 NIV).

One of the bogus (false) premises of certain penologists is that it is no use to attach a stern punishment to the violating of the law, since the normal crook, despite the fact that he knows the punishment (or penalty), will pay no regard to it.

This obviously is sophistry of the worst kind. Many enticed to foul up (to do wrong, sin) have been restrained from committing the act as a result of their insight into the punishment (penalty); and accordingly society is protected.

It is true for course that there are some who are not restrained by the dread of consequences because they delude themselves into believing they are savvy enough to outsmart the law.

It is a stunning thing in talking with those in jail to find the quantity of the individuals who state they gave no idea whatsoever to the punishment when they carried out the wrongdoing. There is an analogy between these foolish men and the those who will stand before the Great White Throne of judgment.

They had found read about the judgment, and maybe even heard it preached - but despite this, they gave the matter no serious heed. Now as they stand before the bar of eternal justice, they are moved with bitter remorse. In any case, for them, as Esau, there is no place for repentance.

They Stand Before God

What power of force unites this incredible huge number before the Great White Throne? They are said to stand and not sitting. The prisoner in a natural (earthly) court when he hears his sentence articulated is required by the court to stand, thus it will be on that great day.

What power causes the multitude to appear before the great throne of authority isn't hard to understand it. It is the same power that keeps the planets in their individual orbits about the sun, or the stars in their courses. The dead have no choice in the matter; the power that raised them from the locales of hades irresistibly sets them before the great throne of judgment. From this there is no conceivable escape. Nor will any hope to escape it.

Every Knee Shall Bow
(Phil. 2:9-11 KJV)

In spite of the fact that the dead stand before God, there is likewise the moment when they will bow the knee. In the heavenly counsels it has been determined that every knee will bow before the Lord Jesus Christ, and each tongue will confess that He is Lord.

This was first alluded to by the prophet Isaiah in chapter 45, verse 23 KJV. The apostle Paul makes reference to it in Romans 14:11 KJV and in Philippians KJV.

"Wherefore God also hath highly exalted him, and given him a name which is above every name: That at the name of Jesus every knee should bow, of things in heaven, and things in earth, and things under the earth; And that every tongue should confess that Jesus Christ is Lord, to the glory of God the Father" (Phil. 2:9-11 KJV).

Now the wicked in their natural pride had hated to bow their knee to the Lord Jesus, and it was their privilege to do as they saw fit. In any case, regardless of whether they condescended to recognize Christ as Lord of all on earth, the hour currently is now at hand when they are compelled to do Him reverence (homage).

This includes things in the earth and things under the earth-a reference to the individuals who had residence in hades. These spirits from hades who are currently raised out of that locale for judgment, will now bow the knee before the Lord Jesus.

Among these will include the great conquerors, Alexander the Great, Julius Caesar, Napoleon Bonaparte, the insidious (evil) Hitler, the proud Mussolini, the atheists in the Kremlin. They will include Herod the Great who looked for the Christ-child's death, Herod Antipas who mocked Him, the men who sentenced Him to the cross, Pontius Pilate who sentenced Him to death. For each knee will bow and each tongue will confess that Jesus is Lord.

Chapter Four

The Books Are Opened
(Dan. 7:10 KJV; Matt. 12:36,37)

THAT HEAVEN HAS ITS records and chronicles is a subject which is not often considered by either Christians or sinners. By the by, nothing is more clear in the Scriptures than the way that God keeps books.

In fact we are informed that our very words are recorded. It is important now to cite the expressions of Christ in Matthew 12:36, 37 KJV.

"But I say unto you, That every idle word that men shall speak, they shall give account thereof in the day of judgment. For by thy words thou shalt be justified, and by thy words thou shalt be condemned."

We are informed that all that we speak, every one of our words are being brought down as though we had an electronic recorder next to us all the hours of our life.

Consider the awe of the sinner who stands before the blazing light of the Great White

Throne. The angel turns on the account of his life, and he hears his past discussions, his reviling, his past conversations, his cursing, his words of contempt, disregard for, disdain and dismissal for the good and the holy.

The man needs no prosecuting attorney to pronounce him guilty, his own words condemn him. Science discloses to us that somewhere down in memory there is a permanent record of all we have said and done. However, at the Great White Throne there will be no lawful details, no shyster legal counselors to distort or make a mockery of justice, no escape clauses (loopholes) to impede justice.

The words and deeds of men, all things considered, which are all faithfully protected in heaven's books, will be the basis by which they will be judged at the Great White Throne. Daniel the prophet alludes to this great judgment scene and the time when the books were opened.

"A fiery stream issued and came forth from before him; thousand thousands ministered unto him, and ten thousand times ten thousand stood before him: the judgment was set, and the books were opened" (Dan. 7:10 KJV).

Judged By Their Deeds
(Luke 8:17 KJV)

To what extent will the Great White Throne Judgment last? It isn't essential for us to set up the period of time, but clearly the judgment won't occur in a split second (not instantly). Each man will be judged. The content does not clarify the details or the courses of action.

We might make certain that the solemn procedure will be adequately, efficiently carried through. Every individual will be judged by what is written in the books. A transcript will be displayed.

Many a dark deed long overlooked, or forgotten will be brought to light (be revealed). Indeed, even as Christ said: "In nothing is secret, that shall not be made manifest; neither anything hid, that shall not be known and come abroad" (Luke 8:17 KJV).

Will The Righteous Stand At The Bar Of The Great White Throne?
(Rev. 20:5,6 KJV)

The above incident would imply that both the righteous and unrighteous will stand at the bar of the Great White Throne. Now we know that the righteous dead of past ages will be resurrected before the Millennium. Those who were martyred for Christ will rule with Him during the 1,000 years of the kingdom age. They had their part in the first resurrection. On the other hand the wicked dead won't live again until the 1,000 years be finished:

"But the rest of the dead lived not again until the thousand years were finished. This is the first resurrection. Blessed and holy is he that hath part in the first resurrection: on such the second death hath no power, but they shall be priests of God and of Christ, and shall reign with him a thousand years" (Rev. 20:5,6 KJV).

So from this may give the idea that lone the wicked dead will stand at the Great White Throne Judgment. Be that as it may, there is an statement found written in Revelation 20:15 that we should give thought. It says: "And whosoever was not found written in the book of life is cast into the lake of fire."

This Scripture announces that everybody not found written in the book of life is cast into the lake of fire. Does it, thusly, suggest that there will be some whose names are found in the book of life?

What about the righteous who die during the Millennium? Now we know we no one who has rejected Christ will be given another opportunity. There is the heaviness of Scriptures against this. "And as it is appointed unto men once to die, after this the judgment" (Heb. 9:27 KJV). Not another opportunity. By the by, there are sure conditions which require our consideration. Shouldn't something be said about the righteous of the earthly race who live during the Millennium?

Plainly death won't completely be conquered during the thousand years of peace. We allude not to the glorified holy people who were raised at the first resurrection and rule with Christ during the Millennium, but to the individuals who are conceived and who live on earth during that time.

People will live and die then, however life span will be stretched out clearly to that of antediluvian days. As we have seen, he who dies on at the age of a hundred will be considered as a child. Common lifetime will reach out to numerous hundreds of years even as "days of a tree." Unfortunately, there will be some who will choose the wickedness during the Millennium. They will come under divine curse:

"There shall be no more thence an infant of days, nor an old man that hath not filled his days: for the child shall die a hundred years old; but the sinner being an hundred years old shall be accursed…. They shall not build, and another inhabit; they shall not plant, and another eat; for as the days of a tree are the days of my people, and mine elect shall long enjoy the work of their hands" (Isa. 65:20,22 KJV).

It is apparent from the passage in Isaiah that the Millennium isn't the perfect age. The righteous who don't have glorified bodies will live for a long time, but in the end they will die. Both the righteous and sinners will live and die.

In any case, since it is appointed unto men once to die and after that the judgment, therefore, won't these who have died during the Millennium, both righteous and unrighteous, stand before God in the judgment? If so, then those who are righteous will unquestionably find their names written in the book of life.

What About Those Who Never Heard The Gospel? (Romans 2:12-14 KJV)

In posing this question, we are not discussing the individuals who have had chance to acknowledge Christ however left it behind, but instead the heathen who have never heard. The question is frequently posed, shouldn't something be said about the those who in their lifetime never heard the message of Jesus Christ and the cross?

Will their adversity of never having had an opportunity to acknowledge the gospel sentence them to everlasting night? Regardless of what answer we provide for this question, we should concur that multitudes who have lived and died never heard the story of Jesus Christ.

What will be the basis of their judgment at the Great White Throne? As was said of old, "Shall not the Judge of all the earth do right?" (Gen. 18:25 KJV). We will not endeavor to take care of the problem involved; it is a perplexing subject. In any case, we will take note of specific Scriptures that obviously bear on the matter.

Paul discloses to us that the individuals who have not had the written law will be judged by the law that is written on their conscience. The individuals who have sinned without law will die without law, and those which have not the law, however do commonly the things contained in the law are a law unto themselves. Is Paul here expressing a standard of divine justice? Let us quote the whole passage.

"For as many as have sinned without law shall also perish without law: and as many as have sinned in the law shall be judged by the law; (For not the hearers of the law are just before God, but the doers of the law shall be justified. For when the Gentiles, which have not the law, do by nature the things contained in the law, these, having not the law are a law unto themselves" (Rom. 2:12-14 KJV).

There are two contested passages in I Peter which numerous Bible understudies accept have a bearing on the dead who have not heard the Gospel:

"For Christ also hath once suffered for sins, the just for the unjust, that he might bring us to God, being put to death in the flesh, but quickened by the Spirit: By which also he went and preached unto the spirits in prison; which sometime were disobedient, when once the longsuffering of God waited in the days of Noah, while the ark was a preparing, wherein few, that is, eight souls were saved by water" (I Pet. 3:18-20 KJV). "For this cause was the gospel preached also to them that are dead, that they might be judged according to men in the flesh, but live according to God in the spirit" (I Pet. 4:6 NIV).

No doubt these Scriptures encourage that Christ after His death went to hades and preached to the spirits who lived in antediluvian days. It is also called attention to that Noah, the only preacher of righteousness, could not have preached to the millions then living.

Obviously there are other interpretations. Some believe the above passages imply that Christ did not actually preach to these spirits at the hour of His death by any stretch of the imagination, however, preached to them through the Holy Spirit in the times of Noah. To be completely honest, we feel that such an interpretation is stressed and hardly does justice to the plain statements of the text.

It would not be in opposition to reason or to God's Word to believe that God has made provision for every man to have one chance. John the Baptist said that Chist is "the true Light, which lighteth every man that cometh into the world" (John 1:9 KJV).

However this will be fulfilled, we don't have a clue. This we know: there is hope for the man who accepts the light when it comes, but there is no hope at all for him who rejects it.

It gives the idea that God figures judgment based on the soul's reaction to light when it comes. All who would be saved must accept the grace of God through Jesus Christ and His shed blood. There is no other name under heaven whereby men must be saved.

Christ owned three statements concerning this subject which are well worth studying. They clearly have a bearing upon how God will Judge man in the final reckoning:

"Jesus said unto them, if ye were blind, ye should have no sin: but now ye say, We see, therefore your sin remaineth" (John 9:41 KJV).

"If I had not come and spoken unto them, they had not had sin: but now they have no cloke for their sin" (John 15:22 KJV).

"If I had not done among them the works which none other man did, they had not had sin: but now have they both seen and hated both me and my Father" (John 15:24 KJV).

God has not called us to hypothesize on these matters. We know His judgments are flawless, perfect. We likewise know that today is the day of salvation, and those who put off accepting the way have no hope for another opportunity in some far-off distant tomorrow.

Chapter Five

Who Will Judge The Wicked
At The Last Day?
(Rev. 20:11 KJV; John 5:22,23, 26,27 KJV)

GOD SITS ON THE throne at the great day. Also, before his "face the earth and the heaven fled away" (Rev. 20:11 KJV). Despite the fact that the Father sits on the throne, He doesn't personally take part in the judging.

Christ, speaking of this in the Gospel of John says, "For the Father judgeth no man, but hath submitted all judgment unto the Son: That all men should honor the Son, even as they honor the Father...For as the Father hath life in himself; so hath he given to the Son to have life in himself; And hath given him authority to execute judgment also, on the grounds that he is the Son of man" (John 5:22, 23, 26, 27 KJV).

Despite the fact that Christ is the judge who will supervise the judgment of the last day, His isn't a discretionary judgment. No decisions will be made that are not already made.

Only the sentence remains to be pronounced. The sinner is condemned already; he is as of now lost. Only those individuals who accept Christ as their Savior are saved. There is no other way of escape. That way is clearly shown in John 3:16, 17 NIV.

"For God so loved the world, that he gave his only begotten Son, that whosoever believeth in him should not perish, but have everlasting life. For God sent not his Son into the world to condemn the world, but that the world through him might be saved."

If the sinner fails to accept the way of escape, there is no hope for him because he is already under condemnation:

"He that believeth on him is not condemned; but he that believeth not is condemned already, because he hath not believed in the name of the only begotten Son of God...He that believeth on the Son hath everlasting life: and he that believeth not the Son shall not see life; but the wrath of God abideth on him" (John 3:18, 36 KJV).

At the Great White Throne there will be no jury pondering or deliberating the case to decide whether the defendant is guilty or not guilty. The sinner's transgression (sin) speaks of his guilt. There is nothing more needed to decide his doom.

The words that Jesus spoke judge him. Jesus Christ appeared on the scene not to pass judgment on the world however, to provide a way of salvation.

Jesus Christ does not pass a personal sentence on the guilty one as an earthly judge may do after he hears the verdict of the jury. The words that Jesus Christ spoke while on earth will Judge the man.

This is clarified in John 12:47, 48: KJV

"And if any man hear my words, and believe not, I judge him not: for I came not to judge the world, but to save the world. He that rejecteth me, and receiveth not my words, hath one that judgeth him; the word that I have spoken, the name shall Judge him in the last day."

Jesus Christ Is Man's Saviour Today – His Judge Tomorrow (John 5:24, 28, 29 KJV)

In any case, Jesus Christ will manage the judgment at the Great White Throne, and in that sense He will be the "Judge."

A story is recounted of a man who was drowning. An onlooker who saw him going down quickly threw off his external pieces of clothing and jumped into the water after him. He arrived at the drowning man just before he was going to go down once and for all.

In genuine danger to himself the rescuer by strenuous exertion figured out how to bring the man shorewards, and in the wake of working with him for some time had the option to reestablish breath into him.

The man who had played out the act of chivalry (heroism) was a judge. A few years after the fact, a respondent was brought under the watchful eye of him to be judged. The proof showed him to be guilty of perpetrating a crime against society. At the point when the man stood under the steady gaze of the judge, he remembered him as the person who years before had saved his life.

Furthermore, he shouted out, "Sir, do you know who I am? I am the man you saved a few years ago. You took a chance with your life to save me out of the water." The judge took a look at the prisoner and remembered him. In any case, he answered, "Indeed, sir, I do know you. On that day I was your saviour. In any case, today I should be your judge." Truly this episode represents well the relation of Jesus Christ to humankind. Today He is their Savior. In any case, tomorrow He will be their judge. Thus, speaking about the resurrection of the righteous and the resurrection of the wicked, Christ says:

"Verily. Verily. I say unto you, He that heareth my word, and believeth on him that sent me, hath everlasting life and shall not come into condemnation; but is passed from death unto life" (John 5:24 KJV).

"marvel not at this for the hour is coming, in which all that are in the graves shall hear his voice, And shall come forth; they that have done good, unto the resurrection of life; and they that have done evil, unto the resurrection of damnation"(John 5:28, 29 KJV).

The resurrection of life will include those who have accepted Jesus Christ. They will never come into judgment. There is also a resurrection of judgment which will be the lot of all who reject Jesus Christ.

No Change Of Law At The Judgment
(Luke 16:31 KJV)

As we have seen, neither the Father nor the Son really judge the sinners at the Great White Throne Judgment. The expressions of Jesus Christ, verbally expressed well before, judge the sinner. This is wise, merciful, and lenient. It would not be by and large only if men somehow managed to confront some future judgment and not know on what premise they were to be judged.

This is an incredible rule of justice embraced by Americans recorded as a hard copy the American Constitution explicitly encapsulated in it an arrangement prohibiting any ex present facto laws on be passed in the different states.

That is, no law might be passed that ought to be retroactive in its application or its punishment.

On that Great Day there will be no new laws influencing heathens; there will be no curve balls at the Great White Throne Judgment. God has only uncovered all His purpose in His Word. The words verbally expressed by Jesus Christ and recorded in the Gospels will pass judgment on the sinner at that day.

The facts demonstrate that many individuals disregard the Word that is written, but that is their shortcoming. As Abraham said to the rich man in hades, "If they hear not Moses and the prophets, neither will they be influenced, however one rose from the dead (Luke 16:31 KJV). Also, how evident! Jesus died, and became alive once again on the third day. But, many won't accept, however the evidence be overwhelming.

Chapter Six

The Book Of Life

"AND WHOSOEVER WAS NOT found written in the book of life was cast into the lake of fire."

(Rev. 20:15 KJV)

The book of life is alluded to from the very times in the Scriptures. Despite the fact that that precise term isn't used in Exodus 32 KJV, there is no uncertainty this is what is implied. Israel had submitted a great sin and Moses was begging the Lord to save the nation.

He said that in the event that it were impractical to do this; let his name be rubbed out (blotted out) of the book. It is a wonderful representation of self-effacing intercessory prayer, and we quote the passage:

"And Moses returned unto the Lord, and said, Oh, this people have sinned a great sin, and have made them gods of gold. Yet now, if thou wilt forgive their sin-; and if not, blot me, I pray thee, out of thy book which thou hast written. And the

Lord said unto Moses, Whosoever hath sinned against me, him will I blot out of my book" (Exod. 32:31-33 KJV).

Obviously, the Lord wouldn't smudge (blot) Moses' name out of the book of life as that would be in opposition to His supernaturally settled standards of justice. In fact, Moses' intercession profited to save Israel the destiny of elimination (extinction).

As a matter of fact the mercy of God, which is one of His incredible attributes, "sought for a man to stand in the gap," so that His anger (wrath) probably won't be poured out on Israel (Ezek. 22:30, 31 KJV). He found such a man in Moses.

Furthermore, may we include that God is searching for such intercession today. Doubtlessly the seriousness of the Great White Throne Judgment which the heathen (sinner) must face ought to impel all believers to God's Word to give themselves as Moses did to intercession.

The fact of the matter is made that sin is of such a frightful nature, that however a man's name is in the book of life, in the event that he abandons God and does not atone, it will make him lose his place.

Jesus stated, "But he that shall endure unto the end, the same shall be saved" (Matt. 24:13 KJV). He also said, "No man, having put his hand to the plow, and looking back, is fit for the kingdom of God" (Luke 9:62 KJV).

What The Bible Says About
The Book Of Life
(Ps. 69:25-28; Rev. 3:5)

On account of the importance of the subject, let us see what the Bible teaches about the book of life. We have seen that God would not remove Moses' name from the book, since he was under the covenant promise.

Prior, Moses had neglected to circumcise his son, which was the seal of the covenant, and on the eve of delivering Israel, he nearly paid a serious penalty for his neglect (Exod. 4:24-26). Be that as it may, in the wake of satisfying the custom or rite of circumcision, Moses came into the covenant relationship.

As Christians we, by accepting Jesus Christ as Savior, we also come into the covenant relationship-through the new covenant of His blood (Matt. 26:28 NIV).

Psalms 69:25-28 KJV has special reference to Judas Iscariot (Acts 1:25 KJV). Of Judas and all who follow his example verse 28 refers: "Let them be blotted out of the book of the living, and not be written with the righteous" (Psa. 69:28 KJV).

Daniel 12:1KJV discusses the offspring of Israel who came into the hour of the Great Tribulation that "around then thy people will be delivered, every one that shall be found written in the book." From this we comprehend that those who will be delivered from the great judgments at the end of the age will have their names written in the book-meaning the book of life.

The Apostle Paul saw no mystery about believers' names being written in the book of life. He makes reference to Clement and "other fellow laborers whose names are in the book of life (Phil. 4:3 KJV), which demonstrates that we don't need to wait until that great day to find whether our name is written there.

All who wish can know for certainty. Certainly, Jesus Christ gives the same promises to those who overcome that He provided for Moses, saying, "...I will not blot out his name out of the book of life, but I will confess his name before my Father, and before his angels" (Rev. 3:5 KJV).

Of Those Whose Names Are Not Found Written In The Book Of Life (Rev. 21:8; Rev. 20:13 KJV; Luke 16:22, 23, 31KJV)

Jesus, in relating the story of the rich man in Luke 16:22, 23 KJV, says "...The rich man also died, and was buried; And in hell (hades) he lifted up his eyes..." (We consider him the rich man for identification proof, however he has lost all.) As Jesus depicts the remorse of the rich man, we see that the condition wherein he wound up in the under districts (nether region) came as a shock to him.

He understood that he was a lost soul. However in his distress he got a handle on with respect to a straw, hoping for some easing of his wretchedness, for some ray of hope (alleviation of his misery), yet discovering none. In the thousands of years that have slipped by since that time, there has been no adjustment in his lot as far as the Scriptures are concerned.

However, at the time of the second resurrection including the evil dead, there will occur an emotional, dramatic change in the location of the rich man's confinement. "...Death and hell (hades) delivered up the dead which were in them..." (Rev. 20:13 KJV).

The Rich man will all of a sudden wind up drawn out of hades. Again his physical body will be reestablished (restored). Yet, it will be a long way from a happy moment. The human spirit wants to be dressed with a body. Be that as it may, however the rich man will have regained his body-all is in no way, shape or form well.

A thousand thoughts race through his mind of life on earth, of his childhood when he got his father's inheritance, and of the days when he lived in extravagance, luxury. Be that as it may, presently how different are his prospects. He passed a thousands of years in hades with other lost spirits. He is familiar enough with the Scriptures to know that judgment lies ahead, though he paid little heed to the alerts or warnings while on earth (Luke 16:31 KJV).

Be that as it may, the peaking snapshot of his gloomy despair is yet to come. The human heart tends or dares to hope against hope, even when all explanation (reason) for hope is no more, gone. Does the rich man entertain a hope that the will be numbered with those who are granted life? Did he not entertain a hope in hades that some way or another at any rate one prayer of his might be answered?

Now as his turn comes to stand before the Great White Throne to hear the final verdict, does he yet have a secret hope, black out as it may be, that his name would by one way or another be found on the pages of the book of life?

Silently he waits as the finger of the chronicle angel keeps running down the pages. And after that as he sees the angel solemnly shake his head, despair in an ultimate form seizes him. His name isn't there! Tsk-tsk, similar to his five brethren who had the law and the prophets, he didn't believe their testimony. And, the unbelieving can have no part in the regions of light; for them is reserved only the second death (Rev. 21:8 KJV).

True, the rich man was a son of Abraham after the flesh, for he called him "father Abraham. "But, by his unbelief he was not the seed of Abraham by faith (John 8:39, 44 KJV). The fate of the rich man is portrayed in Matthew 8:11, 12 KJV

"Furthermore, I say unto you, That many shall come from the east and west, and shall sit down with Abraham, and Isaac, and Jacob, in the kingdom of heaven. But the children of the kingdom shall be cast down into outer darkness: there shall be weeping and gnashing of teeth."

Thus as the doomed rich man sees the salvation of some who were not of the seed of Abraham, he understands that however he is of that seed, he is a castaway. What's more, in this way with him are fulfilled the words of Jesus:

"There shall be weeping and gnashing of teeth." an articulation which depicts the final emotion of despair. For the lost there is no future.

We have used the rich man as an example of the lot of wicked dead. His story is repeated countless times.

The lost evidently get a brief look at the lot of the saints of light (Luke 13:28-30 KJV). Before they descend into regions of everlasting night, they witness the bliss of those who chose the way for holiness and life. They see the glorious future of the righteous. They have the opportunity to consider God's great plan and the joys of those who now participate in the activities of the unfolding ages to come.

Finally they can gauge the outcomes of their folly. What self-implications, what incriminations, what regret, what sadness as those lost spirits now see that their rejection of God's Word and their determination to pursue a course of self-will, now dooms them forever.

It is a nightmare to awaken from and forget? Too bad, it is only too real. The kindest lips that ever spoke have told it to us as it is:

"Enter ye in at the strait gate: for wide is the gate, and broad is the way, that leadeth to destruction, and many there be which go in thereat: Because strait is the gate, and narrow is the way, which leadeth unto life, and few there be that find it" (Matt. 7:13, 14 KJV).

And so for the lost the endless night of eternity begins.

Is Punishment In The Lake Of Fire Eternal Physical Torment? (Rev. 20:10 KJV)

From Revelation 20:10 KJV it is concluded by some that punishment in the lake of fire is eternal physical punishment. From this, medieval scholars (theologians) drew colossal pictures of physical torment past anything brought about by human imagination.

This origination of punishment of the evil isn't correct. In any case both the body and soul will be destroyed in Gehenna, which is the lake of fire. There will be, subsequently, no physical torment.

"And fear not them which kill the body, but are not able to kill the soul; but rather fear him which is able to destroy both soul and body in hell (Gehenna)" (Matt. 10:28 KJV).

We see by this that both the soul and body are destroyed, and only the spirit is left. All out termination, extinction or annihilation isn't inferred, be that as it may, as Christ in Mark 9:43, 44 KJVsays when again referring to Gehenna speaks of "the fire that never shall be quenched, where their worm dieth not, and the fire is not quenched." The implication is that awareness (consciousness) is retained. This warning takes on increased emphasis by Christ's repeating it three times.

The eternal banishment of a human being is for sure a frightful thing to contemplate. But it would be infinitely worse if God somehow happened to give these wicked spirits freedom and permit to occupy and to infect God's kingdom, which they would most likely if they were allowed or permitted entrance.

Sin is the infringement (the violation of) of the law of being. And willful sinning is sure to bring anguish and suffering upon those who persist in it.

Chapter Seven

Eternity Begins
(John 10:27 KJV, 28; Isaiah 57:15 KJV)

To WHAT EXTENT IS everlasting (how long is eternity)? Jesus Christ in several places in the Gospels promised eternal life to those who believe in Him:

"My sheep hear my voice, and I know them, and they follow me: And I give unto them eternal life; and they shall never perish, neither shall any man pluck them out of my hand" (John 10:27, 28 KJV).

The word "eternity," however, is mentioned but once in the Bible, and it is found in Isaiah 57:15 KJV

"For thus saith the high and lofty One that inhabiteth eternity, whose name is Holy; I dwell in the high and holy place, with him also that is of a contrite and humble spirit, to revive the spirit of the humble, and to revive the heart of the contrite ones."

Here the Lord God talks about Himself as He "who inhabiteth eternity." He alludes to Himself as dwelling in the high and holy place, but also with him who "is of a contrite (penitent) and humble spirit."

The new heaven and the new earth usher us into eternity- time without ending. To what extent is time everlasting or how long is eternity? The human mind is completely unfit to understand its meaning. Each endeavor to gauge it misses the mark, it falls short of the objective.

Eternity is infinite, and man has no means, the forever, everlasting time, for computing or evaluating the unending, unable to comprehend it meaning. Certain pictures have been attracted to give us some thought of its unfathomability, however even these are very insufficient.

We are advised to envision the earth to be an incredible ball made altogether out of minute grains of sand. At regular intervals a bird drops by and expels one grain of sand. Over and over after every thousand years another grain is evacuated in like way.

Consider the extraordinary slip by of time that must go before the whole earth is expelled. In any case, when this is at last practiced, that would be just dawn in forever, or eternity (sunrise in eternity).

Or then again think about the sun, an extraordinary ball almost a million miles in distance across, at long last biting the dust in the billions of years ahead and going to cold stone. And after that envision another fowl flying by once like clockwork and honing it's mouth upon it.

At the point when finally after an inestimable pass of time the entire was eroded, still eternity would just have started. Unrefined delineations? Maybe. Surely they fail to begin to depict the length of eternity.

The New Heavens And The New Earth (2 Pet. 3:10-12 KJV; Isa. 51:16 KJV; Rev. 21KJV)

We will make a few of brief comments concerning events that follow the Great White Throne Judgment.

The 7,000 years are now complete: the judgment of the wicked dead is over, and they cease to have any further part in future events. Be that as it may, the extraordinary unfurling of God's plan has scarce begun as eternity is measured. Paul in writing to the Ephesians speaks of the saints' being raised to sit up in heavenly places, whence God "in ages to come" will reveal" the exceeding riches of his grace."

"And hath raised us up together, and made us sit together in heavenly places in Christ Jesus: That in the ages to come he might shew the exceeding riches of his grace in his kingdom toward us through Christ Jesus" (Eph. 2:6,7 KJV).

The old earth and heavens have served their purpose. The earth even today is showing indications of weariness, exhaustion of its assets (Heb. 1:10-12 KJV). God in His generosity is providing a new home which shall endure for time everlasting (eternity). Men today, by means of atomic offices (nuclear agencies), have within their power the means to annihilate (destroy) the earth (Matt. 24:21, 22KJV).

They have learned how to spilt the atom and by means of chain reaction can produce and deliver blasts of practically boundless power (explosion). Great as will be the devastation during the Great Tribulation, man will not be allowed to destroy the earth.

It will remain after the judgments of the Great Day of the Lord to be the home of the people who possess the earth during the Millennium. When, however, the 1,000 years have run their course, the elements will dissolve (melt) with a fervent heat (II Pet. 3:10-12 NRSV). They won't be annihilated, be that as it may, and some way not yet revealed, a new earth will replace the old.

The former things are now passed away, and will be remembered no more. The past is rubbed out (blotted out). Out of heaven will come the New Jerusalem, the Bride of Christ. The Church shall inhabit the city and God Himself will dwell with them.

The communion of the Lord had with man in the Garden of Eden will be completely restored. The nations that inhabit the earth will have access to the New Jerusalem, but their dwelling place will be upon the earth (Rev. 21:24-26 KJV).

Moses in giving his farewell message to the children of Israel said that he had set before them life and good, death and evil-therefore, choose life.

"See, I have set before thee this day life and good, and death and evil...I call heaven and earth to record this day against you, that I have set before you life and death, blessing and cursing: therefore choose life, that both thou and thy seed may live" (Deut. 30:15, 19 KJV).

And Christ said to the people that the narrow way leads to life and the broad way leads to destruction.

"Enter ye in at the strait gate: for wide is the gate, and broad is the way, that leadeth to destruction, and many there be which go in thereat: Because strait is the gate, and narrow is the way, which leadeth unto life, and few there be that find it" (Matt. 7:13, 14 KJV).

Therefore, God grant that we may choose life.

Bibliography

The Holy Bible (1964) Authorized King James Version. Chicago, Ill.: J. G. Ferguson

The Holy Bible (1982) New International Version. Grand Rapids, MI.: Thomas Nelson (Used By Permission)

The Holy Bible (1978) New York, NY.: New York International Bible Society (Used By Permission)

The Holy Bible (1953) The Revised Standard Version. Nashville, TN.: Thomas Nelson & Sons (Used By Permission)

The Holy Bible (1901) The American Standard Version. Nashville, TN.: Thomas Nelson (Used By Permission)

The Holy Bible (1959) The Berkeley Version. Grand Rapids, MI.: Zondervan (Used By Permission)

The Holy Bible (1977) The New American Standard Bible. USA.: The Lockman Foundation (Used By Permission)

The New Testament In The Language Of The People (1937, 1949) Chicago, Ill.: Charles B. Williams, Bruce Humphries, Inc, The Moody Bible Institute (Used By Permission)

The New Testament In Modern English (1958) New York, NY.: J. B. Phillips, Macmillan (Used By Permission)

The Wycliff Bible Commentary (1962, 1968) Nashville, TN.: Chicago, Ill.: The Southwestern Company, The Moody Bible Institute Of Chicago

Bradley, M. & Bradley, C. (2018) The Great White Throne Judgment. Nashville, TN.: Thomas Nelson, Inc (Used By Permission)

lutzer, E. W. (2015) Your Eternal Reward: Triumph And Tears At The Judgments Seat Of Christ. Chicago, Ill.: Moody Publishers (Used By Permission)

Simmons, J. B. (2015) The Great White Throne. USA.: The Omega Triology

Create Space Independent Publishing Platform (Used By Permission)

About The Author

The Reverend Dr. John Thomas Wylie is one who has dedicated his life to the work of God's Service, the service of others; and being a powerful witness for the Gospel of Our Lord and Savior Jesus Christ. Dr. Wylie was called into the Gospel Ministry June 1979, whereby in that same year he entered The American Baptist College of the American Baptist Theological Seminary, Nashville, Tennessee.

As a young Seminarian, he read every book available to him that would help him better his understanding of God as well as God's plan of Salvation and the Christian Faith. He made a commitment as a promising student that he would inspire others as God inspires him. He understood early in his ministry that we live in times where people question not only who God is; but whether miracles are real, whether or not man can make a change, and who the enemy is or if the enemy truly exists.

Dr. Wylie carried out his commitment to God, which has been one of excellence which led to his earning his Bachelors of Arts in Bible/Theology/Pastoral Studies. Faithful and obedient to the call of God, he continued to matriculate in his studies earning his Masters of Ministry from Emmanuel Bible College, Nashville, Tennessee & Emmanuel Bible College, Rossville, Georgia. Still, inspired to please the Lord and do that which is well – pleasing in the Lord's sight, Dr. Wylie recently on March 2006, completed his Masters of Education degree with a concentration in Instructional Technology earned at The American Intercontinental University, Holloman Estates, Illinois. Dr. Wylie also previous to this, earned his Education Specialist Degree from Jones International University, Centennial, Colorado and his Doctorate of Theology from The Holy Trinity College and Seminary, St. Petersburg, Florida.

Dr. Wylie has served in the capacity of pastor at two congregations in Middle Tennessee and Southern Tennessee, as well as served as an Evangelistic Preacher, Teacher, Chaplain, Christian Educator, and finally a published author, writer of many great inspirational Christian Publications such as his first publication:

"Only One God: Who Is He?" – *published August 2002 via formally 1ˢᵗ books library (which is now AuthorHouse Book Publishers located in Bloomington, Indiana & Milton Keynes, United Kingdom)* which caught the attention of The Atlanta Journal Constitution Newspaper.

Dr. Wylie is happily married to Angel G. Wylie, a retired Dekalb Elementary School teacher who loves to work with the very young children and who always encourages her husband to move forward in the Name of Jesus Christ. They have Four children, 11 grand-children and one great-grandson all of whom they are very proud. Both Dr. Wylie and Angela Wylie serve as members of the Salem Baptist Church, located in Lilburn, Georgia, where the Reverend Dr. Richard B. Haynes is Senior pastor.

Dr. Wylie has stated of his wife: "she knows the charm and beauty of sincerity, goodness, and purity through Jesus Christ. Yes, she is a Christian and realizes the true meaning of loveliness as the reflection as her life of holy living gives new meaning, hope, and purpose to that of her husband, her children, others may say of her, "Behold the handmaiden of the Lord." A Servant of Jesus Christ!

Printed in the United States
By Bookmasters